The
Moon
And Other
Failures

The Moon And Other Failures

F.D. REEVE

Michigan State University Press

East Lansing

∞ The paper used in this publication meets the minimum requirements
of ANSI/NISO Z39.48–1992 (R 1997) (Permanence of Paper).

Michigan State University Press
East Lansing, Michigan 48823-5202

03 02 01 00 99   1 2 3 4 5

Library of Congress Cataloging-in-Publication Data

Reeve, F. D. (Franklin D.), 1928–
    The moon and other failures : poems / by F. D. Reeve.
    p. cm.
  ISBN 0–87013–522–0 (alk. paper)
  I. Title.
PS3568.E44 M66 1999   99–6070
811'.54—dc21   CIP

Grateful acknowledgment is made to the editors of the following peri-
odicals in which these poems first appeared: *The American Poetry
Review, Folio, Free Lunch, The Hudson Review, The London Magazine, The
New Criterion, New Letters, The New England Review, Poet & Critic,
Poetry, a Magazine of Verse, Poetry Now, Potpourri,* and *The Sewanee
Review.*

"Alcyone," a modern oratorio for singers, musicians and narrator with
music by Thomas L. Read, had its world premiere at The Barbican, Lon-
don, on 18 March 1998 as part of the "Inventing America" series.

Cover artwork by Kathryn Darnell of Darnell Calligraphy & Illustration
Book and cover design by Michael J. Brooks

Visit Michigan State University Press on the World Wide Web at:
                    www.msu.edu/unit/msupress

for LCS

with love

Contents

Voices

When I hear my lover singing, I sing, too.
    The tune? Something I make up in my head.
Words come and go—wind, mood, mode—
      listening and loving, I sing her what Henry said:
      No one else got music like you do.

The sound of music tells us who is who—
    a patterned mind, shapenotes in the dark,
rhythms (the thunder) pounding down the air . . .
      By pairs we populate imaginary arks
      and climb great mountains to paint a grander view.

Brash and raw like crows in morning rain,
    Achilles' war cry and mad Ajax's lament
pierce my dry heart. When Virgil sings for Rome
      (sings of arms and the man who founded a new race)
      I think of Troy in ashes and of Dido left to burn.

Time lies on the dead as they sleep in each other's arms.
    The celestial harmonies play on unheard.
Here is the day like a warm stone in my hand,
      the earth going round and round on its carousel
      as if, after life, the singing goes on and on.

Lake Champlain

The rocks rise from the water; the wind, from the West.
        Old fables constellate the sky.
The woods are full of spiders. Abenaki ghosts
        in bark canoes glide among the pines.

On the granite cliff we sleep in each other's arms
        under the cast of a mythic spell
by long, sweet summer love made soft and brown,
        waiting for the great lake god himself

to deliver the past into our native hands.
        We dream we are the islands and the water
that sing through the trees of the happy hunting grounds
        where the starry animals are slaughtered

and trapped souls shaking in the morning light
        as in a web spiral off to death.
Awake, we step across our long-lost lives
        stone by stone, breath by breath.

Arthur, Fishing

By the Thames where at breakfast he
      from his picture window supervised ducks
      now came two boys of which one (he
      was no longer sure about boys) looked up
      (saw / saw not through glass: Uther, king)
      then up again and down the river,
      the ducks were there, hen first, the ducklings
      surely less one or two (the pike)
      which his own excited hands had lifted,
      quivering feathers, from the impossible
      crotch of the old apple tree, the boy
      scanned the water, saw fish rise
      or imagined them, turning to the other
      as the ducks like toys along the verge
      between The Unicorn and The White Hound
      glided in sinuous grace,
      pointed to the water as if a hand
      had risen (Caliburn, O legend).

Then with his second cup of tea
      she said, How many are there today?
      But she was always watching the boy:

Then not for love, in no one's image,
      not counting the past, or time passing,
      the unregistered years of the Fisher King
      given over, Arthur gone home for love,
      in a warm kitchen smelling fresh bread,

touched by the white owl's shadow *guenhwyvar,*
while the man recounted his lost ducks
(the pike, the pike!) the perfect boy
thinking like a fish, where the fish was,
unlimbered his line into the damp air,
took his mark, and cast there.

Silence

In May each dawn rolls down the mountain
as backdrop for the birds.
Songs and other acts of passion
      imbricate the woods.

Leaves like overlapping shields
      catch the sun aslant.
Days are shingled up in years,
      and space is layered light.

Sweetened by white apple blossoms,
      the air is filled with bees
stitching flowers into quilted patterns
      for the earth's geometry.

Elephants and carriages—
      summer halts upstage.
Cloud spectacles, like presages
      of circus winds to come,

vanish beyond the silver poplars
      as the music rebegins
and lovers' medleys turn to plainsong
      at sext praising the wind.

In September maples lengthen
    along the barren ground
like the crossed shadows at Golgotha.
    The days start darkening down.

The world moves toward self-consumption,
    as arrogant and blind
as a forest in the frozen silence
    left behind when birdsong ends.

Lapidary the blue sky, the dry autumn
    which we walk through like a dream,
surprised to find Orion hunting
    among the fallen stars each dawn.

Damariscove

The little men have gone who told me life
was a simple story of following the sea.

In bow and stern they sat in hunchbacked silence
as if wrapped in plastic, staring down the fear

that no one has another place to go.
But nothing happened: day after empty day

no keeper rose from the cold black water,
and the waves, like their lives, rolled aimlessly away.

Perhaps some wind removed them. Or their line gave way.
No man can stand up to the winter sea.

Walking the beach, I hear it steal the sand,
and on cold clear nights, its hollow harmonies.

Longings

Front flat as a flounder, man alone,
       upright, the indenture of himself,
   forever searches for his missing half.

Some say the noblest lovers are men loving men—
       pure parthenogenetic nature—
   two heroes yearning for the golden mean.

O brave implausibility! O bold
       and death-defying sacrifice!
   Each ghost casts a shadow like a passing cloud.

My love is hiding in the Wood of Fear.
       She went there hunting for her soul.
   Nothing like it either on the world screen.

When Hephaestus asked the lovers side by side,
       "Do you desire to be one?"
   he took confusion for assent. For their need

he then melted them together, and as one soul
       they wandered the Elysian Fields,
   nodding with love like the asphodel.

Neither living nor dead, stones cannot be erased.
       They exist forever in some form.
   But love, like a stonefly that burst from its woody case

this warm May morning, goes hand-in-hand with time,
      as the idea of me walks with her still,
   and my soul waits for hers where fire makes the bronze shine.

The Moon and Other Failures

The stones of Paris smell of books
   from bibles lighting up the Middle Ages
      to romantic tales of unrequited love.
      Every Sunday my grandfather winds his clocks
      and checks the past for any uncut pages.

Time still presses hard upon his house
   buttoned up against late winter snow.
      The market changed, he'll soon move away
      because suddenly he fears an airplane crash,
      like Montaigne who fled the plague in old Bordeaux.

As I walk along the Paris streets surprised
   by the fanshaped stones and the butt of a Roman wall,
      I fancy Grandpa waiting at a corner
      and wonder if bishops still rise to Paradise
      and every king is picketed in Hell.

Fresh bread on Easter morning would fill the air
   with joy. (The Way of the Cross goes on and on.)
      Meanwhile, the planets pass with cold indifference,
      and documentaries of a thousand wars
      (the latest technologies) compute the sun's

position in the encyclopedia of matter.
   The house of Heaven, like the Luxembourg full of statues,
   with its old families who used to constellate the sky
   burns to ashes. Wandering the streets of Paris,
   no one remembers the moon and other failures.

Telephone

—I put it in for my convenience, he said,
my neighbor, who seldom answers the telephone.
    —Is the Spirit of Communication dead,
I ask him—or you just going it alone?

    On the day he was born, Hermes killed a tortoise,
    pulled off the shell, strung gut from side to side,
        then plucked the strings.
        Later that day
    he rustled fifty of Apollo's cattle,
    hiding their traces by making them walk backwards,
        but an old man saw
        and told Apollo—
        Apollo roared.
    To apologize Hermes sang a song,
    then gave Apollo his new instrument,
        which Apollo loved so much
        that everywhere he went
        he took his singing shell.

    My love's voice fills the air.
    From the far side of the hill it whirls
    like a cloud down the summer wind,

sways like ripe fruit on the end of a branch,
shines like the gold skirts of Athena,
as vast, as rare.

She walks the earth on her arm. The sea
swells in her laughter. She rises in the light
that warms the honeyed pines. Night
after night, she unweaves the remains of the past
into the future's endless story
in a call to me.

Coasting

Adrift in uncollected time
like sailboats invisible in fog,
the extraordinary selves we wanted to become
pretend to keep their daily logs
as the mind courses from sleep to sleep
down an imaginary map
and night after night we plant our homemade flag
        on insubstantial shores.

Because all things balance—as on a wheel—
and we cannot see nine-tenths of what is real,
our claims of self-reliance are pieced together
by unpanned gold. The whole system is a game:
the planets are the shells; our earth, the pea.
May there be no moaning of the bar.
Like ships at sunset in a reverie,
        we are shadows of what we are.

If soul is form and gives a body life,
reality is a gathering of ghosts.
Love, like a magnet, draws each lover out;
the light that speeds around in empty space
extracts the future from the past.
We circle the stars to find our secret place,
and the dying mackerel believe the gong
off Pemaquid tolls for them
        on the cold gray-green sea.

The Club

The rooms are full of ghosts. In the leather chairs
a thousand old men turn the pages of their lives.
On the wall *Henry James at Thirty* shares
the holy patience, having found a wife
unnecessary and his prose a genteel fit.

Downstairs, handcuffed to poverty, black servants
like dark young Decembrists in red jackets keep
through all their union hours a secret allegiance
to a just new world. Upstairs, like sunlight, sleep
steals across the floor from chair to chair.

What if *The Gentleman from San Francisco*
died not alone in Italy but among such friends?
What if one had so many? This winter, though,
what revolution will achieve its ends?
And how can we know who is loved and rare?

Vermont Sonnets

When the selvage of the gray November sky
is fringed with light, and the barren birch by the pasture
shiver like lace in the thin mountain air,
the old house, too, becomes a starker, colder white.

All things left to weather change their nature
as they pass from fall to spring beneath the snow,
before bursting with the fat buds in April's fair,
dressing the world in greenage everywhere.

Today as clouds gather and a northeaster breaks,
the eye of time seems suddenly at hand.
Oh fate is fate, but who can tell from old leaves
or from the shifting sky what shape it'll take?

      Dread what's coming; trim the past with grief—
      in May the heart will rise with the rising land.

This time of year the hills have settled down.
The sky is slipcovered by a leaden cloud
like chairs left to winter in a summer house.
   The dark woods have begun to fill with snow.

War rages on almost every continent,
the radio reports, calculating the toll
from famine and the number killed by shells:
   Text and subtext—always the same intent.

How presumptuous to think we are not who we are
or to imagine forgiveness. By these our hands
we work our praise, although we are condemned
    for so much dependence on the single star

    that rises each morning on the east side
    of the mountain and transfigures the earth with light.

To love or not: Who ever had the choice?
Abelard kissed Héloïse before he fell;
for kindness, Raskolnikov's whole life was spoiled,
damned to stalk itself on the ice of Hell.

Each day driven by divine desire
like the mountain sun to take you in my arms,
I fly to your body for its secret fire
to burn in your arms in a whirl of flammable forms.

The blind and other metaphors go round us
        weightless in space, coralling the speechless stars,
        admonishing the moon and the forward clouds.

The bells of heaven chime the witching hour.
        Then borne on the cool wind that comes up in the night,
        love, tell me a story of delight.

There's a world to talk to; there's also you.
Regardless how I add the matter up,
I find the universe divides in two:
　　each flying saucer wants its flying cup

　　and suns will burn themselves to death because
　　(pygmy despots in their mini-systems)
　　they're plagiarized by gravitational laws.

Peppermint, camomile, coriander, jasmine—
the constellations sleep between your breasts.
The clouds have vanished that were the angels' breath
　　and the falling stars have fallen to their rest.

　　The moon is hushed, and the night is filled
　　with your face like a shadow with a voice
　　whispering across the trembling hills
　　　　Hic locus sacer amoris est.

Betrayed by women, by one woman loved,
　　I came in winter on the western wind,
driven against myself to the bitter mountains,
　　not thinking to be drawn down in the spring.

So much for cold conceit. As the grass turns green
　　and birdsong fils the lilac-scented air,
the earth remembers its natural pretense—
　　time counterpoint—the harmony of things.

White rock beside dark cave—Sorgue River springs
    near Mont Ventoux—with love then leaves the mountains.
(In Avignon Laure caught him on the wind—
    ever after was his only icon.)

    The plague long gone that left her in his mind,
    his lines sing like meadowsweet in the summer air.

At daybreak, shimmering in silver light,
woven in space between shadow and shadow,
a spider web, like a new-discovered star
beyond the Magellanic Cloud,
demonstrates the geometry
of fact that binds the universe.

Beyond lies the garden. Gold carp swim round
the brick pond like whales in an ocean,
as if the border redwood and the Russian pines
were as moveable as fish,
or like Los Angeles some day
transshippable to the Aleutian Trench.

    Each small astonishment
    magnifies the unmade earth
        and its dumb intent.

halis pantessin Homeros
—Theocritus

Because nobody can sign what isn't there,
    the life that goes so fast seems not to show.
Its negatives accumulate like rare
    deposits of depleted ore. And no
late-summer delving or red apples' falling
    makes a sound in this black hole—no name-calling,
no music, no Zeus-driven thunder. A long wall
    of silence connects me to the Otherworld.

Wrong about Fate, driven mad by guilt,
    blind Oedipus found his naked self,
    the murderer he had looked for all his life.
Predict what you will, we live what we have felt.
    Although our dreams, like oracles, seem strange,
    in our real deafness there's no sign for *change*.

Twilight

I walk through the woods at twilight.

                                    A veery calls.

The sun, too, spirals down.

                          The air cools.

The wind is dying that all day

                            swayed the leaves

of the ash and maple

                  like a vast umbrella

and shook the quivering aspen.

                      So many days

to pass through;

            so many lost.

                    Set like a stele

on the next rise,

            a gnarled gray birch

                            lauds the old ways.

I think instead how it grew

                  from so many small lives.

Two Questions
(At a Baptism)

Children,
>   the river was high last night.
Do you hear the struggles of your generation?
The setting sun like a switchblade cuts off the day.
The gods are laid out in their gallery on West Mountain.

The gentle earth is older than you imagine,
going through, while we put coats on in the hall
(your lives and ours are not like the stars' at all)
the light-years separating lunch from dinner.

No one is so beautiful as you
who rose from under the snow, who sing your parts
in earth's festival each spring, acting out
for the faithful your love's transparency of heart.

How will you get on when we have gone?
You walk through our minds in clouds of possibilities
like the outlines of half-remembered dreams.
In the world of illusion, too, we smell of mortality.

On our day in this church of life, we begin at the end.
Before and after our journeys, we all are home,
where lemons are sweet, where hearts and all broken things mend,
and sorrow flows like honey from the comb.

Roller Coaster

How like a set of "Russian Mountains"
space defines our time: days lose, years gain—
the killing avalanche of stones this morning
subtends a millenarian moraine.

Monet's haystacks turning purple
as the sun meets its angle of repose
will segue in the accelerator-future
into anti-haystacks half supposed.

My grandfather's life, like my green childhood,
has faded. So, sunlight fades at five,
and a meadow loses its pastoral likeness
as asphalt spreads and malls thrive.

Coffled together by fear but stony
and silent like the cairns at a summit turn,
we, too, assume contradictory postures,
plunging into the Tunnel of Love.

The One and the Many

The earth is too hot to last
      though each time we tear it apart
      we save the pieces.

Desdemona stirred up the leaves
      as she ran naked through the woods
      in Othello's dreams.

The softness of the first touch
      of Francesca's tongue remained fresh
      in Paolo's memory.

Day after day the sun goes down,
      love; then your hand on my breast
      torches the night.

Catching Up

A long life fades away as the waning moon
      slips from its cusp when the sun rises
      into the blue, unblemished sky.
                     Death is
      endless hide-and-seek, the skull perhaps part
      of a later archeological find, like a Greek spoon.
Starting over would be better: a new heart,
      praise-singing, and fresh cards all around.

Living a year is more than building a house:
      at the end of the past, time now notwithstanding,
      the future threatens, and what you remember
      does not justify profits, the off chance
      of fame, the inevitability of loss.
He denies Hamlet who is the Rosenkrantz
      of the new galactic middle class.

If only there were something to it. If art,
      say, or justice, ever came true.
      If a tree could lean down and unbutton you.
      No torture. No buffalo jumps. No new gods
      competing with you to drive old Phaethon's cart.
So dive like the falling buffalo into the clouds.
      Blow hard on the sun until, like a match, it goes out.

The Village Graveyard

The fallen leaves are red and dry.
Autumn burns. Star Lake mirrors
a blue October sky.
In the cemetery the forgiven and unforgiven
lie side by side.

Hoarfrost on the goldenrod.
On the northern mountains, new-fallen snow.
Time like a kindly god
reserves some open spaces in each row
for the living dead.

How long do we have who follow the sky?
Beneath the rustling maple leaves
in a green plot eleven by five
these ashy bones compact our fond belief
that the sun won't die.

The Death of Achilles

Full moon in Cancer.
Along the shore
the sweat-soaked bodies burn
ever brighter, ever more lonely.

One by one the fires go out,
then the oil lamps on the long boats
drawn up at Troy
on the shelf of the wine-dark sea.

Andromache's women sweep
through the glass bells of memory
like bats through midsummer twilight
feeding on men.

For the hero—games and glory,
the pomps of death. Then also
the cold wash of the sea knocking down the long walls,
polishing the stones like ice.

Full Moon in May

In the gray darkness on the rim of dawn
red-shouldered hawks move out along the river.

    My heart unfolds like moccasin and trillium
    in leafy places where nothing grew all winter.

Kri! Kri! Lords of the air, they tear
small birds apart in natural majesty.

    The ghostly authority that was my father warns me
    from man's point of view no cosmic wind is fair.

Indifferent maples shake their chartreuse leaves
like poplars in each honeyed breeze. The sun rises.

    Life's design: to cut our wood like facts yet
    to enfold the stuff of fancy and one silk belief.

The moon mirrors the sun: there we see
our common face and the fate of every star.

    This morning so much bursts forth that I despair
    of head catching heart. Live winter relics, the trees

gasp for air, and rocks deny the ground.
The sky is bony with the shells of love.

    All around, good people cry to be released.
    The troop of oligarchs waves its goatskin gloves.

The sea, like a plate full of light, tips back and forth
from dark to dark; the violence of the waves—

       see "Aphrodite at the Fifteenth Phase"—
       rises in perfect beauty; and a woman's gaze,

or a witch's, seduces Solomon. The full moon this May
after our last terrible winter washes the lost earth.

Alcyone

When shall I see those halcyon days?
                                        —*The Clouds*

Prologue

In the gray night   a horn
                    green lights
                    wet easterly air.
        The waves sing in the dark.
        The stars hang in the trees.
The wedding on shore is over.
The dinghy slaps
                    small scalloped water.
The weather is fair
                    for the man and his bride
to set sail on the sea.
                    The schooner is waiting,
his handlining ship,
                    the fish-catching *Amaranth*
with his two brother deckhands
                            ready for sea.

Chorus

        Blind with desire
        like raw young lovers
        from behind statues in a public park
        the sailors explode

29

across the lawn
fish scales on their hands,
cold blood on their conscience,
the ship keeled in shipyard
slung like an ox.
Degenerate dancers,
who burns the water to ashes?

Scene 1

Sweet-haired Alcyone sails away, whose skin
is brown and soft like down, whose eyes are black
like silk buttons, who waves good-by
with her small hands as the water rises
and her body bends to the thrust of the sea.
Now she beats east beyond the white rocks
of the bay, where the ocean begins.

O handsome man, she thinks
                    of her sailor,
as she unbuttons her blouse
                    and lets it slide from her shoulders,
and steps from her jeans
                    and her lace-trimmed linen,
folding all neatly
                    onto the shelf
and shaking her hair
                    loose for the night,
at last putting on
                    her rose-petalled gown,

high-cheeked and tall,

        your hair is your crown.

All your green childhood

        did you long for the sea?

Each year did you stand

        back-to-back with your father

until one day you turned

        so you mirrored his face?

Ceyx, for his part,

        sails the gray sea

one hand on the trawl-line,

        one eye on the wind,

knows that beyond

        the brow-bowed horizon

there's the take of her body,

        the sweat and the fish smell,

the pitch and the roll

        of nights of love

                on the open sea.

She moves with wild and natural elegance,

      rare animal of air and earth.

What then pulls them apart?

      Is it the sun all day scorching the sea

when there is no wind and the heaving swells

      roll the boom back and forth,

the sheets drag in the water

      and the galley pots bang together?

Or is it the midnight gale

      that drives them terrified down

forty-foot billows under bare poles,
     the drogue sieving the ocean
and the two of them pinned to the ship,
     their hearts lashed to the sea?

Morning: the pearled horizon like a necklace
     decorates the charcoal water;
     blood streaks the deep blue sky.

Hippasus and Hylas stand watch. High clouds warn
     of weather coming on. Ceyx kisses
     his bride's breasts and takes her in his arms.

Her hair shimmers in the cabin light;
     her head on his chest releases his heart.

Chorus

    Fortune Teller:
        I've seen a black dog that walks like a man.
        It comes as thin as a shadow out of the fog,
        licks your hand and puts you under a charm.
        There's evil in the sea drawing men down,
           Like the spell cast by the drowned.
    Sailor:
        Maybe evil comes out at night with the stars
        disguised to work wickedness as it will,
        but what I haven't seen I haven't seen.
        Women have many desires. They'll sleep
           with a dog if it walks like a man.

Fortune Teller:

    Tell me your passion, sailor,
                (the salt water has softened
                my nails and my fat heart)
    and I'll tell you if Fate'll be kind—
    if the waves'll roll off the rocks
        like silver dice from your palm.

Scene 2

    A ceaseless wind drives the ocean against them.
Thick arching waves, like pods of whales
passing the boat from back to back, push the prow
ever leeward, leaving less and less made good.
Salt stings her much-kissed lips, her high-boned cheeks.
His eyes, like his fish-gutting hands on her breast, grow cold.
"What do you think," she asks as, for a weightless moment
swung on top of a wave, her fingers brush his,
the ship stiffens and the wheel holds,
"of turning back?"
                As wild horses race from hill to hill,
chests lathered, tongues flicking saliva,
lashed by their own invisible wills, so Ceyx
waves her away and puts the wheel over, calling out
to his brothers to haul in the trawl line and keep filling the hold:
"The wind is a transient god, and the sea
speaks a hundred languages. Nobody knows what's next."
He sees her resentful look but doesn't relent,
although she means plainly she isn't a man. The men,
who pretend to ignore her while overhanding the lines,

keenly sense her coming and going, eyeing her hands
as she hooks on the bait, recording the set of her head,
then in their hungry minds undressing her
and covering her body with desire
because it's dark and different and forbidden.
She doesn't know how like a bee from rose
to briar rose she seems to float on sweetness
as if carried by the breeze that spins the foam
and in fair blue weather makes the rigging sing,
or that the golden light she walks in swings,
or that when she passes the honeyed air reminds
a man of fallen pine needles in the sun.

So they who for hours
                            have worked the ship
through heavy air
                            on steady tacks
lose their heads
                      to Envy and Dream,
which come upon them
                                  unawares
each time they look
                            into her black eyes,
enchanted,
                  seduced by their fire,
onetime watchers
                            of the skies
who sense that the sun
                                  does not suffice

and tremble
       for the body of
a woman burning
              to the touch
                    like ice.

Chorus

       Beware of those
       who rage with the sea
       because they owe it their living
       and leave it their dead.

       They turn on each other
       like rats cocking their snoots,
       devouring their children,
       laughing at luck

       cracking the shell
       on the lobster's back,
       pulling the tooth from the shark,
       cutting the flesh off the whale.

Scene 3

              Up from the green water
              that lifts the bow in long curves
              comes Hylas as thin as a wafer
              casting a shadow like silence.

His passion smokes in his eyes.
His aspine body slinks aft,
one hand on the rail beside him,
one hand reaching out in the night.
By the door he checks, then surges
inward, as a cresting wave,
quitting the ocean, curls
over its own dull thunder
the length of the beach and breaks
with a hollow roar. So he pauses,
set, like a stone at the door,
his face broken by the light,
then lunges to his end.

A maiden of the sea, like Senta,
Alcyone lies in the great double bed
for which Ceyx deftly carved the headboard.
In the aureole of the gimbaled lamp
by which she reads a book, her hair
shines like water. Her cheeks and forehead
glimmer with an orange glow.
The handle turns; slowly at first;
then as if blown by a gust, the door opens.
She gasps. She drops her book. She starts
to rise. She sees him standing there.
She lifts her book to shield her breasts.
"What—do you—" she begins, but her mind
replies before she has finished asking.

36

Not tall nor short, nor old nor young,
up from the weeds of faithlessness,
a man who lost his life in shadow,
his shoulders hunched in crippled pride,
he shuts the door and scuttles closer.
His eyes attack in hungry anger,
his hands crawl crab-like through salt air,
while, like a shark's, his body twists
and whips behind his bared white teeth.

She bends with fear, draws back. Her arms
pressed close against her, she binds her thighs.
What he wants takes up her mind:
her thinking knots around her pelvis.
"No!" she cries in disbelief
as if escaping from a dream.
Then she smells his fish-stained clothes,
the seaweed stench, the rotten bait,
the stink of sea-death and decay.
Too late to dress but not to rise,
not to be taken in her marriage bed!
She leaps to the floor, by her stance defying
the madness in his eyes, the two crooked,
clawing, oncoming, slithering hands.

Swaying as the vessel sways,
staggering through the smoky light,
he lours, balks, drops low to dive
beneath the fear in her dark eyes
and her two stiffened, stone-brown hands.
To him she shimmers in her gown,

miragy like the girls he dreams
accessible and bare, each goal
so long desired, so long denied.
Gathering himself to mount,
he drives closer, harder, madder, seizes
her wrists with his rough, reddened hands,
and swiftly, as foul as a rotten god
drowned in a pagan galley come up
for revenge, he bends her back on the bed.

As a minnow pursued by mackerel darts
wildly left and right into the dark,
so she twists her hips against his groin.
His body weighs on her like stone.
She hooks a foot behind his leg,
arches her back, and rolls. He rocks,
but hardly moves. He roars. He chokes
her with her hair and holds her flat.
His forearms pin her shoulders down.
Each time she turns her head he slaps
her face; each time she tries to rise
he digs his nails into her neck,
scratching trails of blood across her skin.

The effort in the blood arouses
him to frenzy. Each time she spins,
each time she tries to knee his groin,
each time she bites or kicks or thrusts,
he, enraged like Cyclops when
Odysseus drove the red-hot stake
into his eye, screams for vengeance,

pommeling her hate-filled eyes,
her flattened, purple-nippled breasts,
her beautiful brown body that almost
belongs to him. He shakes her until
she finally goes limp, and he,
like a great conqueror of the skies,
against the mahogany bedstead carved
by Ceyx as his wedding present,
plunges into her body, pliant in loss
and cool to the touch as in first death.

As a small sloop caught in a sudden storm
tries to work clear of a leeward shore
but, swamped and driven by a merciless wind,
its rudder gone, rigging half-carried away,
is rolled by the waves and smashed on the rocks
and left for scavengers to pick clean in the calm,
so she lay as broken and still as a wreck
on her wedding bed—
                    her world, her home, her grave.

Chorus for Two Voices

>   *Maiden:*
>>   Pass by! O please keep going!
>>   Pass by, barbaric bones!
>>   I'm young! Kind sir, keep going!
>>   Don't touch me! Leave me alone!
>   *Death:*
>>   Give me your hand. You're beautiful and quick!
>>   I'm a friend who wishes you no harm.

Cheer up! Cheer up! I'm not barbaric.
You'll sleep safe and soundly in my arms.

Scene 3 (Conclusion)

In the calm that followed, he rose with hatred
in his heart for having had her favor
and exchanged his own, her possessor now
in life and death-in-life. Who lay
below him with the battened eyes
and matted hair had no patch on him.
He pushed himself away from the cold
brown, rubbery skin. His manliness
towered in its triumph, and his chest
swelled huge and round with greatness.

The scratches on her shoulder, the bloodstains
on the sheet, her bare and flattened chest,
the thin black hairline from her navel
down, her passive thighs apart
as he had left them—and he wondered,
Was that all I conquered?
                                        She lay
diminished in his mind, contempt
like a stain spreading through his blood,
the rage to have turned inward, scorn
as cold and crystalline as ice
stiffening his spine and hands.
Quickly, with a swagger, he belted up,
repeating to himself that she

40

had gotten what was coming to her.
Brother's wife or no, he had done
what men said he had the right to do.
Don't forget, he said to the whispering darkness,
this is what a woman's for.
As a man, hadn't he such power
that she came, too? The bitch, he thought,
to pretend to be satisfied by one man
when anyone else would do. Not his fault.
A woman parades herself like that
is sending out news. Not guilty, he said
to the hissing echoes along the wall;
in fact, from now on she better show
Hippasus and me her gratitude.

He stepped toward the door like an olympian fighter
flashing victory in his eyes
and hearing imaginary cries
and cheers from a tumultuous crowd.
He paused to acknowledge the applause:
silence save for the slap and swish
of the sea as the fish-bellied schooner cut
through the crests of the dark, indifferent waves.
In the cabin, the air was still. Her lips
were parted. Her chest rose and fell
irregularly like the sea.
He stopped, he stepped, then stopped again,
enchanted by her placid face
and the desolation of the room
as if a greater power than he
had taken over, or all along

had worked according to its plan,
or things had happened on their own,
and she all by herself had died.
His haunches tightened, his hands were shaking
again as he remembered the moment
of blinding light. He watched her closely.
Not dead, he thought; look, she breathes.
The whispering walls, the accusing ceiling,
the headboard frowning its reproach,
the bed on which her body floated
as on a tranquil sea mocking him,
threatening him to leave, daring
him to stay, challenging him
to come tomorrow night again—
everything conspired against him.
Why should he stand here dumb as a post
waiting for the sky to fall?
As he turned to go, he said to her
in his mind, Don't forget, I'm your lover now.
He opened the door, expecting the dawn
and the change of watch to come.

Chorus

    Voice 1:

        The sun beats a stone face
        into similes and messages.

    Voice 2:

        Cod, mackerel, plaice
        die in the gray sea off Ithaka
        begging for salvation by grace.

Voice 1:

> The push and pull
> of the tides throws fish in the air—

Voice 2:

> moonstone eyes and women's hair
> as fine as the silk of Cos.

Voice 1:

> Fishermen down the north wind
> from the sea, longing for home,
> the suitors came to Penelope.

Voice 2:

> Her hands
> knitted her voice into the bees' hum.
> Her thumbs closed their eyes.

Scene 4

His hand on the handle, the handle turned.
The bedroom door swung open. Tall
and hard as stone, a living statue
canary yellow in working weather gear,
water streaming down his legs,
his body shaking with thunder, Ceyx
barred the way. "You?!" he roared.
His iron eyes held Hylas fast.
Behind him the sea pounded the schooner
and the waves lashed themselves into foam.
His rage rose relentlessly like the sea.
He seized his brother round the neck
and swore he'd die like a dog if he

had laid a hand—
                    He didn't finish.
Over Hylas's shoulder he saw Alcyone
on the bed. His fury exploded in his hands.
He flung Hylas to the floor like a sack.
"Don't move." Weak Hylas thought to rise;
Ceyx kicked him flat. "Don't move!"
he repeated. "I haven't yet begun."

At the sound of his voice, she called his name
and raised her arms. He kissed her lips.
Her hands closed round his dripping suit
and pulled him to her. "You're wet," she said.
"All wet," he said. He laid his ear
against her heart. "Are you all right?"
She nodded slowly. "I didn't think
it'd ever happen—not one of them."
Ceyx's body stiffened; he glanced at Hylas
crouched on the floor. "Never again," he swore.
"But—look at your cuts—oh god!—tell me,
are you really all right?" She shrugged; she nodded.
"It hurts, the cuts. And in my head,"
she added. "Where is he now?" "In the corner,"
said Ceyx. "Let me heat some water. My fault
that I ever took him on. Don't move
I said," he barked when Hylas put
a hand on the floor as if to rise.
Hylas fell back. The open door
slammed on the wall; the wind whined;
the ship shuddered again. Cornered,
rat-like Hylas started crawling

44

toward the door, shaking, sweating with spite
and ready to swim rather than die.
Ceyx rose in wrath, crazed
like Aias by unjust suffering.

As wild as a shark in a blood-streaked sea
he swung a great arm round Hylas's neck,
then seized his throat and punched his face.
Hylas kicked and rolled, snarled like a weasel
and lunged out the door for the last of his life.
On deck he circled the skylights, as a child
at tag tries to escape around a tree.
So an animal always shows its mind.

The clouds hung low; spume blew in sheets.
Ghostly orange, swaying wildly
like a withered jack-o'-lantern
in the shadows of the cabin light,
Hylas twisted left and right
until Ceyx in gigantic wrath
leapt over the skylight and with his shoulder
pinned his brother to the mainmast shrouds.
A shriek, a hopeless, final cry
like a rabbit in an eagle's claws,
but Ceyx, certain of his course,
struck his brother's useless belly
one salt-stung blow and punched his jaw
once, twice, three times. Hippasus at the helm
like a born observer kept his distance;
not up to him to referee.
Nothing now save Ceyx's hands

held the adulterer up, whose mouth
went slack, whose thin arms flopped, whose knees
downjacked the body to the deck.
When suddenly the ship railed down
and one green wave roiled along the side,
the beaten brother, bent like paper,
was borne off on the waves of the midnight sea.

A phosphorous flash; the wind moaned;
the living looked at each other, and stood down.
The fitful sea heaved underneath them,
drawing great breaths, tossing and turning,
screaming in nightmare, then stabbing the dark
before lying down to the blood-red dawn.
Ceyx's glance, like a hammer, nailed Hippasus to the helm.
He himself went down to the cabin again,
wondering if life would run wildly downwind
without drogue or design, no longer his own,
himself caught in the coils of the saurian currents
        that whirl through the wine-dark sea.

Chorus

    Fortune Teller:
            I alone see the future in its basket.
            I alone see what swims the Sargasso Sea.
            I see fire-red eyes and boiling water,
            geysers, whirlpools, ships a-foundering,
                    monster fish devouring men.

Sailor:

You're making that up because you don't know
the sea's made of salt, bitter and strong
when a nor'easter blows, full of mortality.
Sure, we pretend that life's a dream,
    but everyone knows every body goes down.

Fortune Teller:

Show me your money, sailor,
and I'll put the world in your hands—
I'll give you the black-eyed bones
    you love to roll from your palm.

Scene 5

Lying on her side, Alcyone cried,
her forehead furrowed and her lips drawn tight.
Ceyx stripped his jacket off, knelt down.
He touched her head and gently rubbed her back.
"Where does it hurt most?" he whispered, kissed
her ear. She shivered and began to sob.
"Here," she said, laying his hand on her heart.
His eyes ran down her silken face, across
the hollow where her neck and shoulder met
to her hand on his beneath her sweet brown breast.
O Al, o friend, long-fabled love, it was
my fault. Didn't I lose as much as you?
"When I came in and saw him standing there,
I thought he'd killed you. I listened for your heart
but only heard my own," said Ceyx softly.

He kissed her cheek and said he'd heat some water
for surely it'd be good to wash. "Vengeance,"
he laughed, "drove Cain mad. It did me, too."
As the water heated, he began to tell
how Hylas was at first too scared to move
but then ran off as nimbly as a rabbit;
how he caught him at the shrouds and knocked him out;
then the great sea did its work as it always does.

      With faithful eyes she watched his expression change.
"He slipped away as he was meant to go,"
he said, "so quick there was nothing I could do."
Nothing you wanted to, she thought, aware
that she alone was left with *him* and no way
to wash the memory of his touch away.
She heard her voice singing in the sea,
the wind her breath, and the constellations strung
across the sky like ribbons through her hair.
How small her body; how small herself inside.
Faultless, how far she fell: What was her flaw?
Ceyx's voice echoed in the distance.
She felt his square hands wash her neck, her shoulders,
her arms and body, her sullied groin, her thighs.
He dressed her cuts, and combed her hair, and said,
"The hawks that feed on summer songbirds have
a selfish, jealous look. That snake in the Garden—"
She laughed. "Wait," she said. "Let me do the snags."
She reached up and drew him close. He took her in
his arms, but the movement pierced her chest with pain
and cut her breath. She winced; she groaned; he caught
her hands in his and brought them down. "Not yet,"

48

he whispered, bending low. "It was no one's fault,"
she said. "It just happened, like a rainy day."
He erased her frown with his thumbs and kissed her lips.
"Noah thought his newlyweds safe at sea."
"But suppose," she said, remembering the small
red mole beneath Hylas's left eye,
"suppose it was laughable as well?"
Suppose, she thought, *you try to save yourself*
but then suddenly find your body detached, like a moon,
a sort of weightless object whirling round
your head? That's wild enough. But wilder still,
you lose all feeling and childlike see
the little ironies—the crowsfeet by
the eyes but not the fury, cuts and marks
on the skin but only afterward its sweat
and slug-like slime. "I mean, isn't life absurd?
Who could prevent something so ridiculous?"
She didn't mention that, like a ghost beneath
the cabin sole, an image stalked her memory,
its gray teeth clacking, its rotten breath on her face,
its hands reaching for her neck, its thumbs
tightening, tightening although she kicks and twists,
saliva running from its mouth—and then
the small red mole underneath its eye
as blindly the violence becomes perverse
and her world recedes into a black hole
and the starry sky turns as pale as an illusion.
"I mean," she said, "what difference would it make?"

"If I had thought—" he began, broke off, thinking,
It makes all the difference, but I can't say that.

"What's done is done," she whispered, catching up
his thought. "Neither can *Amaranth* sail backward."
"My fault—my blindness—that I took him on,"
said Ceyx truthfully, wanting to give her all
the time she needed so his hands, like a dream-catcher,
could net her terror, and she'd remember the past
with fondness and look to the future unafraid.
He wondered how soon the outer scars would heal,
how long the inner one would stay. What lie,
he asked himself, could now absolve her pain?
Slowly, changed by her change, he felt the distance
between them, decided to bridge it. "Give me your hand,"
he said, hoping to bring them out of themselves.
"Just the touch of your hand tells me I'm alive."

       She reached to touch his face. He took her hand,
kissed her palm. Such quiet love, she knew,
was now as far as they could go, afraid
her bitterness henceforth would be a part
of how she walked and talked and thought, clear
in the secret current of her electricity.
For Ceyx, she knew, the violence was real
but not the violation. He wasn't diminished,
not even by failure, of which—save bad luck fishing—
he hadn't had any. "Of course, we'll go on," she said,
"like *Amaranth* herself. Give me time." She raised
her head, asking for a kiss. "A kiss?"

       "All you want," he said and kissed her warmly
as if to solve the ambiguity
although the image of his brother on her

rankled, and he cursed the darkness in his heart.
He meant to be more generous than he was.
Soon we'll waken from this nightmare, she thought,
and find ourselves together at the altar
in the big striped tent or in our bed the night
we first made wholly wedded love.
"Remember?" she said. He kissed her forehead,
cheeks, her hands and lips and stroked her hair.
She pressed her lips to his, fell back exhausted,
and shut her eyes. He watched until her breath
came evenly, then rose, cleaned up the cabin,
put out the light and went to take the helm.
The circle of their little life seemed closed.

      The ship kept pitching through the blue-black sea
as if it, too, were part of nature's pattern
and not a fishing vessel fraught with human
passion, bearing them uniquely forward
into space and time—that inscrutable design
the two of them in fear and ignorance called love.

Chorus

    We are the daughters of Atlas,
        who carries the world on his back.
    We were pursued by Orion
        and all of us changed into stars.

    We are the seven sisters—
        some of us slept with Zeus
    and gave birth to some of the gods,
        and some of us share our names

with others not related.
   That's why if you want to keep track,
please note our sister's unmarried
   and stays with the rest of us stars

to rise in the morning for summer
   and on winter mornings to set.
Not she but the fabled bird,
   the sea-conceiving alcyon,

a-nest seven days before
   the solstice and seven after—
O Halcionii!—
   calm the wind and water.

Some say a kingfisher's beak
   will take the wind's direction,
but we are the Pleiades,
   and we make no predictions.

Scene 6

The voyage lengthened.
    The eastern and the western
stars changed places.
    Day by day the Dog Star
of morning twilight
    yielded to Regulus,
the Lion,
   as round and round in hollow space
the Earth and Sun pursued each other.

52

                                        The fish
in frenzied schools
                    dived deep into the sea.

One night Alcyone
                    at the helm beheld

a ghost:
            Out of the spray across the bow
it rose by the foremast
                        and floated down the deck,
phosphorous sparkling
                        in its seaweed hair,
its eyes as white
                    as the belly of a shark.
It passed like a shadow
                        through the main
and, skimming the ocean
                        like a petrel,
vanished in spoondrift
                        above the waves.

She screamed from fear,
                        then clutched her throat.
The sea kept up its soughing:
                        the ship
broke the waves
                    and the water rained leeward.
The wind sang a high-pitched hum
                                in the shrouds.
Then a second scream

                  poured forth from

her soul

         as if drowning in Phlegethon's blood,

or demons were whipping her

                 naked through Hell.

Ceyx ran to her,

            shouting,

                "What happened?"

Her body shook.

           She pointed.

               She tried to speak,

but, seized by the vision,

              nothing came out.

"Did you see something?

             What did you see?"

"Him!"

         She fell back in her husband's hands.

"He walked through the sail," she said.

                  "Down the deck

first,

      he passed through the sail

              on the water.

His eyes were porcelain

            and his hair sparkled

like the sea

         when you stir it in the dark."

Ceyx hooked the helm

           to hold course,

then bent to her

         to lift her, trembling,

himself not yet believing

                what

he hadn't seen.

            He stepped to the ladder.

She shook with fever

            as he took her down.

"He walked

           across the waves," she whispered,

"from crest to crest

           as down a path.

Do you think he came

           to reclaim his life?"

She felt

       he came for her again.

Ceyx replied,

       "He's gone on to the next.

That's enough of him.

           He drowned."

"But I saw him!" she cried.

             …"Not really," he said.

"You saw, like, a shadow,

           a shadow of nothing,

a trimmer that haunts

           the house under the sea.

It won't come again."

           "How do you know?"

"What claim has it got

           on you or me?

It saw you;

          it knows how the story ends."

"Don't leave me," she said.

　　　　　　　"Sometimes I pray—"

She didn't finish.

　　　　　　"Prayer," he said softly,

"and a fair wind

　　　　　　are the best hope we have."

He stroked her back

　　　　　　and kissed her cheek.

"Rest.

　　　　Close your eyes.

　　　　　　　Let me finish your trick.

It'll soon be dawn,

　　　　　and the ghost will sink

like a scrap of paper—

　　　　　　for that's all it is—

with the other night shadows

　　　　　　　in the western sea."

Chorus

　　Fortune Teller:

　　　　Inside my crystal ball I lift

　　　　　　the moon above the hill.

　　　　A man is in the garden. A woman

　　　　　　waves from the window sill.

　　Sailor:

　　　　The ship that was running to Heaven is now tacking

　　　　　　to Hell. Each wave is as hard as a berm.

　　　　　　Who called home 'The Land of No Return'

　　　　and wrote on the edge of the chart *Here Be Dragons*?

Fortune Teller:

    The briar roses by the sea
        are salt-white. The wind is still.
    She's walking to him through dew-wet darkness,
        stiff in her lunatic will.

Sailor:

    What's rising in the ball like giant fish
        from the soul's center up toward the light?
    Are they his friends, their faces dark,
        their bellies white
    and streaked with blood, feeding the dragons?

Scene 7

The fishing is poor.
    The weather worsens.
        She craves
release from her vision
    and the end of late summer storms.
"He won't leave me alone.
    There's no place on this ship
where I can escape,
    not even filleting the fish.
Twice in the middle of night
    his watery eyes
and his mouth with its stinking breath
    have borne down on me.
I wouldn't have told you but,
    as fishing is bad
and the weather worsening,
    I think we ought to go home."

"Granted," he says,

                  knowing she speaks the truth:

His luck has turned.

                As after lightning strikes

close by,

          the smell of brimstone fills the air,

so now the wind brings on a sour stench

like garbage burning.

                "Who knows why?" he says.

He puts the helm over

              and swings the schooner round.

"Next time—" he begins,

              but she interrupts him, saying

as she slips into his arms,

              "It already feels different."

As if she were a mermaid with bare breasts

or some courtesan,

            like Venus, floating on

the sea,

        she lifts her lips to his with love.

The gods preserve the equilibrium

between man and nature;

              so, when the sea churned up,

Hippasus said it was Poseidon showing anger

for his brother's death.

              "He shouldn't be," said Ceyx,

"because it was a death that no one planned

and therefore was no one's fault.

              But fault or no fault,

the crime was his, and his,

                        the punishment!"

To himself, Hippasus thought,

               If only she weren't here,

none of this would happen.

                   To Ceyx he said,

"You're right.

             The sooner we get home the better.

Until we do,

         you and I must stick together."

The vast, indifferent ocean became their prison.

By day the sun gave cold, gray light.

                      Thick clouds

concealed the stars.

           Their instruments defined

their point, their place, their time,

                but not their purpose,

nor the saltion of the premeditative sea.

Waves pounded the hull.

           The schooner bucked day and night.

The homebound heart

          that leapt to picture the harbor,

where once the striped tent stood

           and the future lay

peacefully

      like a mountain lake at evening,

shrank and dried

      like a man in an open boat.

The storm became a gale.

                              Fresh water mixed

with salt blew slantwise down the deck.

                                      The lee

awash,

              foam swirling past the cabin ports,

Ceyx shortened sail

                    (O loving man

riding down the unforgiving sea!)

but to what point?

                      The ocean stiffened his hands.

Wave after wave

                broke over the bow.

                          The schooner

began to go down

                under the scurf of the sea.

Caught on the crest of each wave

                            as if struck on a rock,

minutes lasted for hours,

                    and hours seemed days.

Their small consolation

              was the idea of home

that shimmered

            like an oasis

                  behind the storm.

There the bed would be warm

                and the clothing dry,

and they'd dine

            on rare beefsteak and raspberry ice.

"Look out!" cried Ceyx

            as the bow dug deep

and a wall of water
    as from a broken dam
swept down the decks
    and over the cabin, too.
The small ship shuddered,
    dipped low to starboard,
rolled to port,
    then hung,
     a swinging pendulum,
on the summit of the ink-dark sea.
      "Ceyx!"
she cried by the main cabin hatch
      as the water flew past.
"Ceyx!"
    She reached out both hands,
      but as fast as it came
he was gone.
    A yellow flash in her eye—
      "Ceyx!"
The wheel turned by itself.
     The place where he stood was bare.

Chorus

  Madness at sunrise—
    there's mortal danger:

 host and communicants
   stiff at the altar;

 the prophets silent
   in heavenly space-time;

cherubim-seraphim
   robed in gravity;

rose-fingered dawn,
      the ultimate warning:

the owl undone,
the lovers speechless
      in their acts of love.

Scene 8

Day after day he who stood at the helm
had held her, had been there for her to hold,
but now even the wind rushed through her arms,
which had nothing in them, like her soul,
its point and purpose lost, too small
and weak to put down the hungry sea.
The ring, the ring! She swayed to the rail
and hurled a preserver at the crest of a wave
as if throwing herself in her wedding ring,
for nothing moved on top of the water
but shadows and foam, shadows and foam.
The ship lurched. She turned. Up and down,
the helm spun left, then right, as the ship
on its drunken course came up and fell off
and staggered into the wind again.
Lost. Neither the cockpit lantern
nor the slowly rising morning twilight
lit up a head on the hopeless sea.
Hippasus take the dory? She do a jibe?

The great pull of the sails, the rudder's kick
were too strong. The sheets would run through her hands.
Surely Hippasus would refuse to risk his life
for his brother, saying, You never can tell
what'll come next on the treacherous sea.

She laid hold of the helm but it thwacked her palms
and twisted free, impertinent,
like herself, to all but its captain's hands.
She saw those hands coming toward her, felt them
again slide around her and draw her in
to their arms. Was Hippasus asleep in his berth?
Flat and cold, like the salted fish, she thought.
No place now for her; no way to live
with him; let him sail the fish home.
Here was her home, her ghost and Ceyx's
asleep in the mahogany bed,
anemones for eyes, their legs
twined like weeds in the ice-cold, blue-black sea.
She shook each time the ship came down
and turned her back on the bow, rejecting
the world that had once lain so bright ahead.
The green-and-white tent came back to her mind
with the whole wedding ceremony, the words
and the dancing, the cake, the laughter, the nights
of love that followed, as if the schooner
were tacking calmly back and forth
beneath the cover of the world
steered safely by *his* two loving hands.

What was that voice? Was the water talking?
Was she imagining the sound?
Was he calling from the waves, Come?
Were his hands rising from the surface,
waiting for her, beckoning, Come?
Was that the back of his head, now turning,
his face, his eyes above the waves
imploring her to hurry, Come?
Good-by, she thought, to *Amaranth*.
She drew her jacket close around her,
made sure her boots were tight. She stepped
to the rail and reached for the waiting hands.
Cocooned in dreams and memories
of love, she dived deep
   into the inevitable dark,
   and the great dark rolled with her
   as it has rolled for five billion years.

Chorus

  Cold the winter day
    you left us. Your body
  sank to the bottom as opaque
    as sea glass.

  Icicles on the shrouds,
    Death beckoning to Hell:
  your soul sailed downwind
    against its will.

64

Drowned in love, sea nymph,
     Alcyone our myth,
the ocean flaps like a tent
     in the sun, without faith.
Loose skies skid out of space;
     lost earths look for a place;
let our song make loving safe
     so that

     amidst our arms as quiet you shall be
     as halcyons brooding on a winter sea.

About the Author

For the first thirty years of his life a resident of the Middle Atlantic states and for the next forty, of New England—the last twenty-five in Vermont—F. D. Reeve has published more than two dozen books of poetry, fiction, criticism and translations. From his home in the Green Mountains he commutes to Wesleyan University where he is a professor of letters. He has received an Award in Literature from the American Academy of Arts and Letters and the Golden Rose of the New England Poetry Society. Recently, a USIA Speakers and Specialists Grant took him to Russia for the sixth time on a reading and lecture tour.